EDGE
BOOKS™

ANIMAL
FACTS OR FIBS

KRISTIN J. RUSSO

Edge Books are published by Capstone Press,
1710 Roe Crest Drive
North Mankato, Minnesota 56003
www.capstonepub.com

Library of Congress Cataloging-in-Publication Data
Library of Congress Cataloging-in-Publication data is available on the Library of Congress website.
ISBN 978-1-5435-0205-3 (library binding)
ISBN 978-1-5435-0209-1 (paperback)
ISBN 978-1-5435-0213-8 (eBook PDF)

Editorial Credits
Editor: Lauren Dupuis-Perez
Book Designer: Sara Radka
Production Specialist: Kathy McColley

Image Credits
Getty Images: CHBD, 21 (top), Christina Krutz, cover (wolf), EyeEm, 10, Flickr Open, 22-23, Gabrielle Therin-Weise, 13, guenterguni, 6, Kerrick, 20, Moment RF, 17, 18, spooh, cover (moon), background, Tier Und Naturfotografie J und C Sohns, 11, ultramarinfoto, 14; iStockphoto: adogslifephoto, 26, ALesik, 15, Andrea Izzotti, 16, Antagain, 29, aureapterus, 27, Caron Steele, 12, ewastudio, 24, back cover, GlobalP, 22, Kaphoto, 21 (bottom), LuCaAr, 9, proxyminder, 28, Saccobent, 25, Smileus, 7, Utopia_88, 19; Newscom: Keystone Pictures USA/ZUMAPRESS, 8, picture alliance/blickwinkel/H, 4

Graphic elements by Capstone Press and Book Buddy Media.

Printed in the United States   5316

TABLE OF CONTENTS

Naked mole rats eat their own poop. The roots and tubers they eat are tough to digest the first time around. The food needs to make another trip through the digestive system.

WILD DISCOVERIES IN THE ANIMAL KINGDOM

About 500 million years ago, an ocean covered most of what is now Canada. A strange sea creature with 50 legs swam in it. About 90 million years ago, a huge bird-like dinosaur laid a nest of eggs in what is now China. Scientists study these **extinct** creatures. They also learn about animals that live on Earth today. One example is the naked mole rat. It spends its entire life in darkness. This animal is not naked. It is not a mole. It is not a rat either. It is an unusual, bald, pink rodent that is nearly blind. The naked mole rat burrows and tunnels underground. It never sees daylight. Special hairs on its body help it know where it is going.

Scientists estimate that there are about 8.7 million different **species** of animals on Earth. There are 6.5 million species found on land. About 2.2 million live in the ocean. To study them all would take about 1,000 years.

Animal scientists try to discover all they can about the animal kingdom. As researchers learn more, they discover what is fact and what is fib about some of the world's strangest creatures.

extinct—no longer living on Earth
species—a group of animals or plants that are similar and can produce young animals or plants

CHAPTER 1

GORILLAS

Gorillas live in family groups called bands or troops.

Gorillas are mammals. All mammals have backbones and grow hair. Female mammals give birth to live babies. They produce milk to feed their babies.

Gorillas are large apes that live in Africa. Mountain gorillas live in mountainous areas in Rwanda, Uganda, and the Democratic Republic of the Congo. Lowland gorillas live in central-western areas of Africa, away from volcanic mountains.

Gorillas have ways to communicate with each other. They thump their chests, howl, and cry.

Gorillas can speak to humans using American Sign Language.

Evidence

Gorillas sometimes look and act like humans. Gorillas' vocal cords are not like those of humans, so they cannot speak. Some scientists thought that gorillas could learn sign language. Then gorillas could communicate with humans. They did experiments to find out.

IT'S TRUE!

Gorillas are mostly herbivores. This means they like to eat plants such as bamboo shoots and fruits. Western lowland gorillas will also eat insects.

Answer: FACT

Dr. Francine "Penny" Patterson began working with a gorilla named Koko in 1972. Koko lived with Patterson during this study. At first, Patterson taught Koko signs for "food," "drink," and "more." Then she taught Koko signs for "love," "good," and "sorry." Koko learned more than 1,000 signs during a 10-year experiment and study.

For a while, Koko had a gorilla companion named Michael. Michael also learned to communicate with American Sign Language. He learned about 600 signs. Michael passed away in 2000.

Today, Koko lives at the Gorilla Foundation in Woodside, California. Patterson visits her every day. They continue to speak American Sign Language to one another.

Penny gave Koko a little kitten. Koko called the kitten "All Ball" in American Sign Language.

Grizzly bear mothers usually give birth to two babies at a time.

Grizzly bears are big. One of the biggest grizzly bears ever recorded weighed about 1,200 pounds (544 kilograms). It lived in Alaska. It stood about 10 feet (3 meters) tall on two legs. Most grizzly bears weigh between 350 and 800 pounds (159 and 363 kg). They stand about 7 feet (2.1 m) tall.

Grizzly bears once lived in western North America from Canada to Mexico. Now they live mainly in western Canada. There are also special areas reserved for them in several states in the United States.

Grizzly bears eat a lot of food. They will eat almost anything, including berries, flowers, wild vegetables, and grass. They also eat insects, rodents, and fish. Grizzlies will even attack larger animals for food.

In the winter, food is harder to find. Then grizzlies have no choice but to eat less. Many people believe grizzlies **hibernate** in winter to survive long periods with little food.

• •

hibernate—to spend the winter sleeping or resting

FACT OR FIB?

Grizzly bears enter a deep hibernation state during the winter.

Evidence

Grizzly bears have traits to help them through the cold winter months when there is not much food to eat. They go into a very deep sleep. Their heartbeat slows to eight beats per minute. They do not drink or pass waste. Their bodies use their own stored fat for **nourishment**. They even turn their own urine into protein! Does this qualify as hibernation?

IT'S TRUE! The largest bear ever recorded lived 12,000 years ago and was called the short-faced bear. It was twice the size of bears today. It was about 12 feet (3.7 m) tall while standing.

Grizzly bears eat a lot of salmon to build up their fat for the winter.

Answer: FIB

Grizzly bears are not true hibernators. True hibernators, such as ground squirrels and wood frogs, stay asleep for the entire winter. This is not true for any species of bear, including grizzlies.

Instead, grizzlies enter a state of deep sleep called **torpor**. They get ready for torpor by eating a lot of food in the fall. They can live off stored body fat during the winter. When they enter their dens, they stay there for most of the winter. Their heart rates and body temperatures drop. Even though they are asleep while in torpor, they will wake up if they hear a loud noise or sense danger.

Grizzly bears will also leave their dens in winter on warm days, but they will go back in quickly. Bears also take care of their new cubs while they are in their dens. This means they are in a light sleep and are aware enough to take care of their young.

. . . .

nourishment—food and other things that are needed to live and be healthy
torpor—inactivity resulting from lack of energy

Polar bear cubs are usually twins. They are often born in November or December.

Polar bears live in very cold **climates**. These fierce hunters are the largest species of bear. They measure 3.5 to 5 feet (107 to 152 centimeters) tall when they are on all fours. When standing on its hind legs, an adult male polar bear can reach more than 10 feet (3 m). Polar bears are also heavy. They weigh 775 to 1,200 pounds (352 to 544 kg). Female polar bears are about half the size of male polar bears.

FACT OR FIB?

A polar bear's fur is white.

Evidence

Polar bears live in one of the coldest environments on Earth. Their long, thick coat of fur keeps them warm. It also helps them blend in with the ice and snow around them. Most people would describe a polar bear as a large white bear. And they certainly are large. But are they white?

climate—the average weather of a place throughout the year

Answer: FIB

Surprise! A polar bear is actually a black bear. And its fur is not really white. It is colorless. The polar bear's outer coat is made up of hairs that are hollow. The shape of the hollow hairs scatters light and makes it appear colorless. When the sun hits the bear's transparent hair, it gets trapped inside the hollow part of the hair. When this happens, the trapped light emits light beams that make the fur seem bright white.

The polar bear's black skin helps it absorb heat from the sun's warming rays. Its black skin and layer of fat are what help to keep it warm in the frigid climate where it lives.

A polar bear's nose is very powerful. It can smell a seal on the ice from 20 miles (32 km) away.

IT'S TRUE! Polar bears can swim more than 60 miles (100 km) without stopping to search for food. They can also swim up to 6 miles per hour (5.2 knots).

CHAPTER 3

MARINE ANIMALS

There are many different types of dolphins in the Red Sea off the coast of Egypt. People have been known to swim with them!

Marine animals live in the ocean. There are many different species of marine animals, such as fish and sea turtles. Some marine animals are mammals. Marine mammals breathe air and give birth to live babies. Like land mammals, they produce milk to feed their young. Many believe that marine mammals are the most intelligent sea animals.

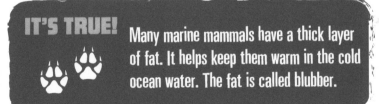

IT'S TRUE! Many marine mammals have a thick layer of fat. It helps keep them warm in the cold ocean water. The fat is called blubber.

Scientists know dolphins have a special whistle sound that they make. The whistle sound is different for each animal. Scientists wondered if this is the dolphin way of calling each other by name.

FACT OR FIB? Wild dolphins call each other by name.

Evidence

Since the 1960s, scientists have thought that certain dolphin whistles were important. They noticed that dolphins in **captivity** responded to the whistles of other captive dolphins they knew.

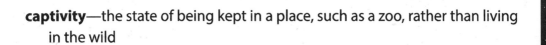

captivity—the state of being kept in a place, such as a zoo, rather than living in the wild

Smaller dolphins eat smaller fish such as herring, cod, and mackerel. Larger dolphins eat larger sea animals such as seals, sea lions, and even sea turtles!

Answer: FACT

Dolphins use unique whistle sounds to address each other. A new study done by animal experts at the University of California, San Diego, suggests that dolphins respond to their names. It's as if they're taking roll call.

Scientists also recorded dolphins whistling each other's "names." They played the whistles for dolphin populations in a different location. The dolphins did not respond at all to the unfamiliar whistles.

Scientists think that being able to identify and call one another by name helps dolphins in the ocean. It is very hard to see in the dark ocean. Sound is important. Dolphins can call out to each other to ask for help or simply to find out where their **pod** is.

pod—a group of marine mammals that live and swim together as family members

Scientists believe more than 440 species of sharks live in the ocean. Different species of sharks have different ways of breathing. Many people believe that sharks must keep moving in order to breathe. They think sharks live in constant motion.

FACT OR FIB?

Sharks must keep swimming in order to breathe.

Evidence

Sharks do not have lungs. They take in oxygen through their gills. Gills are the fish version of lungs. Fish cannot breathe without them. When water passes over the gills, oxygen is taken in.

IT'S TRUE! The three most dangerous sharks are the Great White Shark, the Bull Shark, and the Tiger Shark.

Answer: FIB

It is true that some sharks must keep swimming in order to breathe. These sharks breathe with a system called ram **ventilation**. They draw water over their gills by swimming very fast with their mouths open. Great white sharks, mako sharks, and whale sharks breathe this way. They will die from lack of oxygen if they stop swimming.

The way sharks force water over their gills is different depending on the species. Some sharks do not swim with much energy. Their movements are slow. Nurse sharks and bullhead sharks have developed a breathing system called **buccal** pumping. This means the mouth muscles draw water into the mouth and over the gills. These sharks can breathe even while not moving. Some sharks can switch between buccal pumping and ram ventilation. This depends on how quickly they're swimming.

Great white sharks do not commonly attack people. They attack only 5 to 10 humans per year.

ventilation—the movement of air
buccal—having to do with the mouth

The violet-backed starling and other song birds have one toe facing backward and the other three facing forward. This helps the bird perch on narrow branches. It can even sleep while perching and not fall down.

Many young children are warned that they must not touch a baby bird that they find on the ground. A baby bird touched by human hands is supposedly "tainted" by the smell of the human who touched it. This will cause the mother bird to reject the baby bird. The baby bird will surely die.

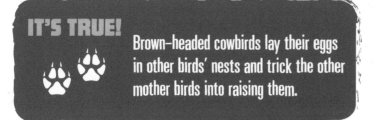

IT'S TRUE!

Brown–headed cowbirds lay their eggs in other birds' nests and trick the other mother birds into raising them.

Baby blackbirds are ready to leave their nest about two weeks after they are born. They learn to fly about a week after they leave the nest.

FACT OR FIB?

Touching a baby bird will cause the mother to reject it.

Evidence

Baby birds go through different stages. Nestlings are very young, featherless baby birds. They can be blown out of their nests on a windy day. Sometimes a storm can bring a whole nest down. Fledglings are a little older than nestlings. They have fuzzy feathers. Fledglings may be out of their nests because they are learning to fly.

Answer: FIB

Nestlings will not survive out of their nests. If the nestling is not injured, it can be placed back into its nest. Its mother will still care for it. Most birds do not have a strong sense of smell. Mother and father birds are not aware of human scents left on baby bird feathers.

The first thing to do if you find a nestling on the ground is locate its original nest. If the nest is damaged, collect as much of the nest material as possible. Put it in an open container and place the container in a tree as close as possible to where you found the nestling.

If you find a fledgling on the ground, just leave it there. Fledglings may not be expert fliers, but they are ready to explore the world outside of their nests. Unless it is in a dangerous place, such as near a road, a fledgling will probably be fine. Its parents will watch over it from tree branches overhead. They will take care of it even if it is not in the nest.

CHAPTER 5

REPTILES

Crocodiles are large **reptiles**. They are found in tropical regions of Africa, Asia, the Americas, and Australia. The largest crocodile is the saltwater crocodile. It can weigh up to 2,000 pounds (907 kg). The smallest type of crocodile is the dwarf crocodile. It weighs only 40 to 70 pounds (18 to 32 kg).

Crocodiles are **carnivores**. They usually eat fish, birds, frogs, and small sea creatures. They will attack any animal splashing about nearby. This includes humans.

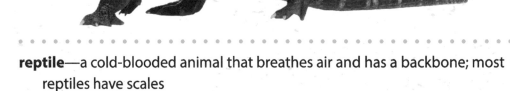

reptile—a cold-blooded animal that breathes air and has a backbone; most reptiles have scales

carnivore—an animal that eats only meat

FACT OR FIB?

A human should hold a crocodile's mouth shut if attacked.

Evidence

A crocodile can be a scary animal. Crocodiles living in captivity are trained to perform tricks showing an animal trainer's ability to hold its jaw shut. These acts can be entertaining. But could they also be helpful if someone was attacked by a crocodile in the wild?

In Africa and Australia, there are several hundred crocodile attacks on humans per year. Up to half of these attacks are fatal. It would be helpful for a crocodile victim to be able to hold the crocodile's mouth shut. In reality, this may not be a reasonable option.

Answer: UNDECIDED

Some animal performers are trained to hold a captive crocodile's mouth shut to entertain an audience. But even they sometimes get hurt. In the wild, a very strong person might be able to hold a crocodile's weak jaw muscles shut. But it is very dangerous and not something people should try. Crocodiles thrash about when they are held down, and a person could easily lose their grip on the animal.

Experts say that it is best to try to outrun a crocodile. A crocodile can swim faster than a human. It can also run very fast. But humans have more endurance to run for longer periods of time. If a person is near the shore, his or her best chance to escape is to run away.

IT'S TRUE! Crocodile skin covers bony plates called osteoderms. They make the skin so strong it can stop bullets.

CHAPTER 6

AMPHIBIANS

The fire salamander is a popular pet, especially in Europe. They can live about 30 years.

Salamanders are **amphibians**. They live in the water and on land. Amphibians are born in the water. There they breathe with gills. As they grow older they develop lungs. Then they are able to spend much of their time on land.

IT'S TRUE!  Salamanders are carnivores. They eat worms, slugs, and snails. Some larger salamanders will eat fish, frogs, mice, and even other salamanders.

amphibian—a cold-blooded vertebrate animal of a class that is comprised of frogs, toads, newts, and salamanders

FACT OR FIB?

Salamanders can grow back their limbs if they are lost or injured.

Evidence

Most salamanders look like a cross between a frog and a lizard. Their bodies are long and slender. Their skin is moist and usually smooth. They have long tails.

There are about 500 species of salamanders. These species can be very different. Some have four legs while others have two. Some have lungs while others have gills. Some salamanders don't have lungs or gills — they breathe through their skin!

Tiger salamanders got their name because they are striped like tigers.

The axolotl salamander is critically endangered.

Answer: FACT

Salamanders are small and easy targets for attack. Snakes, birds, frogs, fish, skunks, and other animals eat salamanders. Salamanders have a **defense mechanism** to survive these attacks.

Different salamander species have different ways of defending themselves. Not all can grow back all limbs and tissue that have been damaged, but some can. Some species of salamanders can shed their tails during an attack and grow a new one. The axolotl salamander can grow back limbs or even organs that are damaged.

defense mechanism—a special method for defending oneself from an attack

CHAPTER 7

HONEYBEES

Honeybees have five eyes—three small ones on the top of their head and two in front.

Scientists estimate there are more than 1 million species of insects on Earth. Insects can be found in every environment. Among the most important of all insects is the honeybee.

Honeybees are needed to **pollinate** flowers so that new plants will grow. Without pollination, plants would not be a reliable food source for humans and other animals.

Some people become beekeepers and keep hives. They look after the bees that live in the hive and eat or sell the honey. Responsible beekeepers always make sure to leave the honeybees enough of the honey they produce to survive and thrive.

pollinate—to transfer pollen from plant to plant

FACT OR FIB?

A honeybee dies after it stings something.

Evidence

Many people are afraid of honeybees because they believe that honeybees sting. They are correct. Honeybees do sting. A honeybee will only sting when it is frightened or its hive is threatened.

Answer: FACT

Once a honeybee stings, its stinger is lodged in its victim. The bee cannot pull the stinger back out. It also leaves behind part of its digestive tract and muscles and nerves. It is this major injury to its abdomen that kills the bee. Other stinging insects don't die when they sting. These are insects such as yellow jackets and hornets. These insects have a different type of stinger that they can pull back out of their victims.

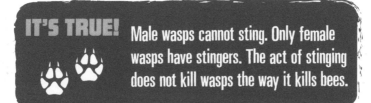

IT'S TRUE! Male wasps cannot sting. Only female wasps have stingers. The act of stinging does not kill wasps the way it kills bees.

GLOSSARY

amphibian (am-FI-bee-uhn)—a cold-blooded vertebrate animal of a class that is comprised of frogs, toads, newts, and salamanders

buccal (BUK-kul)—having to do with the mouth

captivity (kap-TIV-ih-tee)—the state of being kept in a place, such as a zoo, rather than living in the wild

carnivore (KAHR-nuh-vohr)—an animal that eats only meat

climate (KLY-muht)—the average weather of a place throughout the year

defense mechanism (di-FENS MEK-uh-niz-uhm)—a special method for defending oneself from an attack

extinct (ik-STINGKT)—no longer living on Earth

hibernate (HYE-bur-nate)—to spend the winter sleeping or resting

nourishment (NOR-ish-ment)—food and other things that are needed to live and be healthy

pod (POD)—a group of marine mammals that live and swim together as family members

pollinate (POL-uh-nayt)—to transfer pollen from plant to plant

reptile (REP-tile)—a cold-blooded animal that breathes air and has a backbone; most reptiles have scales

species (SPEE-sheez)—a group of animals or plants that are similar and can produce young animals or plants

torpor (TOR-por)—inactivity resulting from lack of energy

ventilation (ven-tuh-LAY-shuhn)—the movement of air

READ MORE

Gagne, Tammy. *Polar Bears Matter.* Bioindicator Species. North Mankato, Minn.: Abdo Publishing, 2016.

Gray, Leon. *Amazing Animal Communicators.* Animal Scientists. North Mankato, Minn.: Capstone Press, 2016.

Lonely Planet Kids. *The Animal Book.* Lonely Planet Kids. New York: Lonely Planet Kids, 2017.

National Geographic Kids. *Weird But True Animals.* New York: National Geographic Children's Books, 2018.

INTERNET SITES

FactHound offers a safe, fun way to find Internet sites related to this book. All of the sites on FactHound have been researched by our staff.

Here's all you do:

Visit *www.facthound.com*

Type in this code: 9781543502053

Check out projects, games and lots more at
www.capstonekids.com

INDEX